re: f (gesture)

re: f (gesture)

poems

Percival Everett

re: f (gesture)

Cover art by Percival Everett

Book design by Michael Vukadinovich
Cover Design by Mark E. Cull

The Series Editor thanks
Elias Wondimu and Tsehai Publishers for their assistance.

ISBN: 1-59709-057-3

Library of Congress Catalog Card Number: 2005933602

Published by Red Hen Press
www.redhen.org

The City of Los Angeles Cultural Affairs Department, California Arts Council, Los Angeles County Arts Commission and National Endowment for the Arts partially support Red Hen Press.

First edition

For HYT

Contents

re: f (gesture)

(ZULUS)

A is for Achitophel.
It was he who put Absalom
up to the big naughty.
Dryden called Achitophel
a great wit. Not to
Blow Dryden off, but the
wit was Solomons's.
Sawing a babe in two?
"And thin partitions do their bounds divide."
So, A is for Solomon
for there are better for S,
because Solomon was small
and a little queer.
A is for Aristotle who
learned from Plato.
A is for Anaximander who
said that the element of
things is Boundless.

B is for blood.
The river of life.
Blood River, where
three Boers were slightly
wounded on 16 December 1838.
Three hours of battle,
leaving three thousand Zulus dead.
16 December, the birth date of
Beethoven, inspired by the
short Napoleon to scratch out
the dedication of Eroica.
B is Bonaparte who lost
three hundred thousand
troops in Spain.
B is for Bound to have a revolution.
B is for the Boston Massacre
which was a media event.
B is for Byron in Greece.

C is for Cicero
who tells that Plato
died at the age of eighty,
"pen in hand."
C is for Chandler, Happy
because he is caucasian.
He sings about "darkies in the field"
before twenty-three thousand
white faces while black men
wait to play ball.
Plato would not have liked Chandler.
C is for costive
because that is what evolution is.
C is for Christ who would not
have approved of Plato.
Happy Chandler is saved.
C is for conceptus.

D is for dreams.
In the Bible, Daniel knew much
of the business of dreams.
Dreams are often deferred,
spiraling round and round,
creeping through generations.
D is for the dead, who
know the value of such dreams
that lurk deep in our
dark history.
D is for democracy,
"the destin'd conquerer, yet treacherous
lip-smiles everywhere
And death and infidelity at every step."
D is for the den of lions
from which Daniel was led *Dei gratia.*
The Divine is not frequently
so disposed.

E is for Earwicker,
the eternal scapegoat,
listening to insulting
soo-wees through a keyhold.
E is for Eros, the first
four letters of "erosive."
Ecce signum.
"Oh, that I should give up my heart
That very special and essential part."
E is for Ellison
and his optic white,
sitting invisible on the outside
edge of history,
watching what can never be his.
E is for Earwicker.
His will be done.

F is for the feathered thrust
and the birth of twins.
Leda never felt a thing,
penetrated by the *force majeure*,
a trick in the air.
F is for fuck.
Finis coronat opus.
F is for Frankenstein,
who did not name his baby.
Always name offspring.
"*De donde vienos, amor, mi ninos?*"

G is for Ganymede
whom Zeus carried, eagle-clad,
far to the top of Olympus,
taking him *en route*.
A feather up his cap.
G is for gluttony.
G is for Garvey
and Gabriel and some in
Guyanna, keeping
"distance from the thickening center."
G is for 'Grab your ankles, America.'
Receive the goods.
The gift is a goose from God.
G is for sodomy.
G is for Goya, who knew.

H is for Hades
who, fearing loss
of gainful employment,
had his bully brother strike
dead Asklepios.
The good doctor was
no friend to the human race.
H is for *haut gout*,
but the stain is not slight.
H is for the law of Hardy and Weinberg.
"*Nam tua res agitur,*
paries cum prmimus ardet."
H is for horrors,
so full of them we dine,
for humanity,
on bent Kantian trees,
for Haqqah.

I is for ichor.
" . . . there is no soundness in it;
but wounds, and bruises,
and putrefying sores;
they have not been closed."
I is for Isaiah,
for the Indian Reorganization
Act. "If ye be willing
and obedient, ye shall eat
the good of the land."
I is for Imhotep.

J is for the journey.
"Like pilgrims to the appointed
place we tend . . . "
J is for juju, for jism, for jazz.
Bebop.
J is for turning your back.
" . . . poetry out of being invisible . . . "
J is for justice, for jabberwocky.
"*Nemo repente fuit turpissimus.*"
J is for Jack
who shall have Jill.

K is for kiss
and what a kiss from
the beautiful twin.
"Sweet Helen, make me immortal . . . "
K is for immortality,
loaded warm about the heart,
an awful weight
and a bad idea.
Hades would agree.
K is for killing,
oft times kindly done.
K is for kiss.

L is for *lusus naturae.*
"Let the living creature lie."
L is for Lazarus
and the Jesus favor-joke,
for Lot and that city
by the bay, for Leibnitz
obscenely grabbing his
monads in public.
L is for "the Lilliths
oft I feldt" and again
Solomon.
L is for Lascaux.

M is for matter and mass,
for mammon piled high
against a greedy sky,
for the many things she gave me,
for Maryam.
M is for maroon
and a swamp or forest
in which to hide,
for Mecca, for mulatto,
for men who meet their maker.
M is for mala'ikah,
for muses,
for the meek.

N is for *novus ordo seclorum,*
that prophetic adornment,
that frightening revelation . . .
"the number of his name."
Always name offspring.
N is for natural, sharper flats.
"In music the passions enjoy themselves."
Nights without melodies
kill without conscience.

O is for owning things
" . . . demented with the mania . . . "
a bad idea in general.
O is for orphan.
Somewhere ova the rainbow.
For ostinata.
"*Entia non sunt multiplicanda*
praeter necessitatem."
Occam on now.
O is for obeah.
Do you believe?
O is for ought,
what you get when
you mix water with an is.

P is for peace,
for Porteus who counted all
too well, for pudding
wherein lies the proof.
" . . . inwardly ravening wolves . . . "
What is the difference
parasitism and predation?
P is for population
and the density therein
affected.
A "pathos of distance."

Q is for eQuine.
"*Quadripedante putrem sonitu*
quatit ungula campum."
Q is for questions,
even if uttered in Greek
by snakes, though without them
there are no lies.
So, all is quiet.
Quite.
Q is for Quine
and paradoxes and so
for Zeno getting nowhere fast.
Z is taken.

R is for rubato,
for the religious
conversion of the Negroes.
Let visions of the afterlife
bind your hands
and take your years.
" . . . moth and dust doth corrupt . . .
thieves break through and steal . . . "
Despite the defeat of
Robespierre.
"*L'homme est ne' libre,*
et partout il est dans les fers."

S is for Shaka.
The water Zwide
I can't get over,
but crossed nontheless.
S is for soldiers
and slaves. Stono.
S is for Sappho.
" . . . with blind ghosts
Flitting, a Nothing, a bodiless shadow . . . "
For secrets, always
alive on the tips of tongues.
"Stolen waters are sweet . . . "
Somesphere ova the rainbow.

T is for what the hedgehog knows.
"*Dat ist der ewige Gesang.*"
T is for time,
that dart throwing arbitrator
which promises eternity
no injury, the great
question beggar.
And so for harmony, stolid,
sensuous and tense-restless.
Fot Tatlin, constructivising
visions of towers
never built.

U is for Anaximander's Boundless.
For Upanishads, oh Maya,
oh Maya, how high the skya.
Thether her umbilically
from the planet and
float her out to space.
U is for Urban II's call
for the big and nasty bloody.
In the Name of God,
und so weiter.

V is for vacuity
and eyes in hollow heads.
V is for the vanities of religion,
for vespertine strolls
through valleys of death
and full of bones.
"*Et vera incessu patuit dea.*"
And oddly, for Verner's law,
voiced fricatives grating
against ears, a poor
variant for music.
"Mock on, Mock on . . . "

W is for word,
for wall, for standing witness,
for wake.
"*Man wird oft von
einem Wort behext.*"

XY is for xylography.
Cut the flesh and
leave the wood alone.
And for xylophone—
“The nights are wholesome;
then no planets strike.”

Z is for Zulus.

(Body)

The Hyoid Bone

Brace the words, the delicate instrument,
the tongue for sweet kissing, upsilon.

Arch of bone, greater cornu, reaching,
reaching, stretching above the lesser.

Fracture this bone, by the violence and
feel the sick pain of swallowing.

Fracture this bone, compromise the support,
and feel the true anguish of speech.

The Sternum

Level, centerpiece of the table of my chest,
find the median line, locate my heart.

Oblique in inclination from above and
downward, forward, it is my shield.

Convex on anterior surface from side to side,
concave from above and downward.

Manubrium, gladiolus, ensiform, come together,
absorb the world through compact tissue.

The Astragalus

Bolster the tibia, that vertical post,
support all of it, pushing against gravity.

The footfalls down the grade are heavy strides,
so receive the blows, the echoes throughout,

through the triangular facet, concave for
articulation with the external part, the connection.

But there are no non-articular surfaces,
but still the echoes find voice in ligament and fiber.

Orbicularis palpebrarum

Lend us a wink, she says, give us a wink,
with that little sphincter muscle about your eye.

Wrap around the ball, around the lid,
from the frontal bone, from nasal process.

Thin and pale, concentrically curving,
covering the eyelids, surrounding the orbit.

Send us a wink, thicker now, with that
sphincter, with that muscle around the looking.

Tongue

The fibers of muscle run in assorted directions,
divided, as it always divides: extrinsic, intrinsic.

Halved symmetrically, it tells a another story
on the other side of the fibrous septum.

The extrinsic muscles originate externally,
only the terminal fibers contained in the organ.

The threads of either half find their interuptions,
full of interposed fat, supplied by nerves.

Palmar fascia

The tree, spreads out to my digits, my satellites,
beneath calloused swellings over the transverse ligament.

Squeeze unconsciously when I am a baby,
give gently when I am a man, control my thumb.

Let my greeting be broad and expansive, firm
and protect my bones which break so easily.

Move my pointings and help me count,
count the years and resist all contraction.

Obturator internus

Partly within the cavity of her pelvis, arising
from the inner surface of the anterior and external wall,

it is attached to the descending ramus of the
os pubis and the ramus of the ischium

Behind the pelvic brim, thrusting from the upper,
arising also from the inner surface at the posterior,

completing the arch, the canal for passage,
where fibers converge rapidly, backward, downward.

Fissure of Sylvius

Where in my head do the breaches meet,
defining the parietal lobe from the temporal.

Sylvius joining Rolando at the tortured frontal,
where the crying starts, where the crying stops.

Beginning in a depression, an interior, perforated
space situated within, it moves out of the hemisphere,

pushes forward a limb, a short acending finger,
upward, inward into the frontal convolution.

Nasal fossae

Pear shaped apertures, opening in front, terminating
behind, by the posterior nares in the naso pharynx,

I smell your sex, pressing through the outer nose,
filling my upper and central septum, brushing my bone.

Deflected from the mesial plane, one side increases,
the other diminishes, unequal only spatially

and deep inside, your sex still drives, finding
the blind pouch, the wall of cartilage, and more.

Sclerotic

Opaque, firm, hard, the way you describe my eyes,
but tell me they are not mean, my love.

Unyielding fiber has served me and left me
alive for you here, now, behind the globe, this shield.

Brilliant and smooth, the ball of your sight,
your vision, the inner surface therein.

Behind it, pierced by the optic nerve,
the tunic dresses the sense you so please.

Labyrinth

Hollowed cavities of bone, the labyrinth conatins
the clear liquor Cotunnii, the twisting trail within.

Complex maze, one puzzle embracing another,
the sound contained in petrous bone, read

through membranous contortions, tracing through
matter and misgivings and remembered hurts.

Semicircular canals mock incompleteness,
returning the sound to the medium without.

Copora Cavernosa

Body of and body without, curved against itself,
consisting of two fibrous, cylindrical tubes, side by side.

It is connected, intimately, along the median line,
in a filamentous envelope, longitudinal, circular

like the movements which cause the changes,
the internal threads filling, strings elastic.

Fibers, fibrils, elongated cells, bands, chords,
trabeculae, muscle, arteries, nerves, fibers.

Larynx

The great vessels lie patiently on either side,
the triangular box, flattened behind, organ of voice.

The pomum Adami is a vertical projection,
subcutaneous and more distinct in me than in my love.

Her throat is smooth and her organ lies narrow,
placed higher in relation to her cervical vertebrae,

bounded, in front, by the epiglottis, behind, by cartilage,
it whispers, it calls, it cries, it makes those sounds.

The Dura Mater

Dense and inelastic, fibrous, lining the inner
wall of my skull, thick where the headaches live.

The outer surface is uneven, fibrillated,
clinging to the inner veneer, opposite sutures

there at the base, the smooth insides.
Four processes press inward, into the cavity,

supporting, protecting, prolonged to the outer
skin where the irrevocable dreams evaporate.

The Weight of the Encephalon

My head hurts the way it hurts,
weighing in at fifty-two ounces soaking wet.

The pain weighs as much, just more than 3 pounds,
rolling like a great round stone from floor to roof.

Fifty-two ounces, an ounce for every card
in the deck which I shuffle in my seeking.

Thirteen ounces for every eight hours,
during which I trace the topography with a match.

The Fissure of Rolando

Convolutions on either side of the line tie
movements of the opposing extremities, on a trace

carried across from the root of one auricle,
passing up, curving back between fontanelle

and parietal eminence, but near the lower end
lie the controls for my mouth, for my tongue,

the tongue she tells me she loves near,
and in, and on, and around her sweet fissure.

Tunica Vaginalis

While I still resembled a fish, the pouch
dropped from my stomach into my scrotum.

By a distinct crease it connects the testis
with the epididymus, the inner surface free

smooth, covered by a layer, tissue of the heart,
the upper portion long since obliterated,

though it may be seen as a fibrous thread
lying loose in the areolar tissue around my cord.

Labia Majora

Posteriorly lost in the neighboring integument,
between areolar tissue, sweet fat, vessels, nerves.

Downward from the mons Veneris to the anterior
boundary, they are cutaneous folds, salient, enclosing,

each with two faces; outer—pigmented, covered by
crisp hairs, inner—smooth beset with sebaceous follicles,

extending together, connecting skin between them,
they press gently past vulval orifice, toward her anus.

The Epigastric

The stomach before, filled with sweet air,
supplying all that lies in the cavity, sitting

before the aorta, the diaphram, expanding
with the motion of life, it surrounds the Coeliac axis

and root of the mesentric artery, downard
to the pancreas, outward to the suprarenal capsules,

receiving small and large slanchic nerves,
semi-lunar ganglia, on either side, squeezing breath.

(LOGIC)

1

We do here
what we do
in a host of familiar cases.
Ask about relations,
about the thing named.
Recall the picture
of that thing.
Tell me which way it points.
Tell me its color.
And whether it can
be broken into pieces.
A queer conception,
sublime logic.

2

Let us assume X.
Even such signs have
some place, some
language X.
Constituent parts
compose this reality—
molecules, atoms, simple
X.

3

Does my memory
of you consist in parts?
Simple, component parts?
Ascending and descending
segments, your
curve in space.
Are you a composite?
Or are you whole,
your name,
all of you at once,
a simple element?
In spite of your
long fingers, your
olive skin, your
perfectly small breasts.

4

The thing must be!
It might be destroyed,
but it must be.
There are samples
of colors somewhere
in a case, standards
like weights and measures,
preserved in Paris maybe,
like the meter, sealed
in a case where
no one can see them.

5

From rags and dust
a rat is formed in the cellar.
It was not there before.
Only rags and dust.

6

Seven men
can be obliterated,
burned or hanged
or drowned in a lake
and forgotten.
Men gone, but
not seven.
Seven men lost,
but not *seven.*
Seven is, will be.
All men will die
but not seven.